THE RELUCTANT
SOLOIST

THE RELUCTANT SOLOIST

A DIRECTOR'S GUIDE TO DEVELOPING CHURCH VOCALISTS

Debra R. Tyree

Abingdon Press
Nashville

THE RELUCTANT SOLOIST
A Director's Guide to Developing Church Vocalists

Copyright © 1994 by Abingdon Press

All rights reserved.

This book is printed on acid-free, recycled paper.

Library of Congress Cataloging-in-Publication Data

Tyree, Debra R.
    The reluctant soloist : a director's guide to developing church vocalists / Debra R. Tyree.
    p.   cm.
    Includes bibliographical references (p.   ).
    ISBN 0-687-00656-2 (acid-free paper)
    1. Choral singing—Instruction and study. 2. Choral conducting.
I. Title.
MT875.T97   1995   94-32545
783.2'171—dc20   CIP
                                                            MN

Illustrations by Charles Cox

94 95 96 97 98 99 00 01 02 03 — 10 9 8 7 6 5 4 3 2 1

MANUFACTURED IN THE UNITED STATES OF AMERICA

To all of those with whom I have been able
to share my joy of music ministry;
with my husband, David,
in my local church,
in the Virginia Conference, and
in the Fellowship of United Methodists
in Worship, Music, and Other Arts

Contents

CONTENTS

Introduction

I have been involved in church music since I was old enough to sing. I have had incredible experiences when I knew that the Spirit of God had filled me and I was able to sing God's Word with new understanding. I also have had my share of horror stories!

One of my horror story memories involves a solo/trio I sang during the first month of a new job as a church soloist. The other soloists were already griping about it because they were all voice majors at the local university and I was a junior in high school. I had been asked to learn the soprano solo and trio portion of the "Agnus Dei" of Schubert's Mass in G. I remember standing in front of the choir with the members of the trio and beginning to sing, only to be stopped by one of the other soloists, who informed me very loudly, "The word is not pronounced like the woman's name, Agnes, but like this: ahhh-nyoooose." I truly prayed to the Lord to open up the choir-room floor and swallow me whole! After rehearsal, the choir director walked me to my car and talked with me about learning more about solo singing. He was caring and supportive, and re-emphasized to me that I had a gift that only needed to be trained and that he was willing to do the training. He reminded me that he wouldn't have hired me if he hadn't thought I had something to offer to the choir and to the worship service of that church. He even suggested that I consider looking into church music as a career. In reality, that was the beginning moment for this book and in many ways the beginning of my journey into church music ministry.

This text is written primarily for the music leadership, the music director or pianist/organist of the local church. I truly hope that you will encourage your soloists to read this as well. Many of the ideas and much of the information can be learned by the soloist directly from this text.

Soloists, I hope that you will read this text and begin to understand a sense of the call God has given to you to share your gift. It is there, you know. It may need to be developed and practiced, but your gift is one to be shared with others. Read the parable of the talents in the Bible (Matt. 25:14-30) and think about what you have to offer to your church worship services. Hold your director of music to his or her call to enable you to use your talents and gifts to the best of your ability.

That is what this book is all about: sharing and caring together as we work to use all of our gifts and talents in worship and praise to God.

Chapter One
Solos and Soloists

Whew! The first night of adult choir rehearsal at a new church! Actually, everything I had planned had gone well, and I was really feeling good about the whole rehearsal and about this new job. Then, one of the bass singers walked up to me and very firmly said, "You know, of course, that I am the bass soloist." Quite honestly, I was confused. As part of my discussion with the interview committee, we had discussed that there were no paid soloists or section leaders. What was this guy talking about? Not more than five minutes later, two more people—a soprano and an alto—also informed me that they were the section soloists. I remember plastering a strange smile on my face saying I would get back with them and then wondered what had I gotten into! After a little research and discussion with the minister and a few other key leaders in the church, I discovered that the previous director of music of the church had decided who was to be the soloist for each section and that was that—literally! Those singers who had come up to me after rehearsal truly had been designated the soloists of the church. The only reason that I had not met the tenor "soloist" was that he had moved with the choir director!

As I drove to church the next week I honestly wondered if I had missed something the week before. I thought I had heard several really well-trained voices and many more voices just waiting to be developed in my choir rehearsal. Had that been a figment of my imagination? By the end of the next choir rehearsal, I knew that I had not imagined the potential in the voices in my choir! There were gems waiting to be polished in that choir room. I just needed to talk them into wanting to be polished and then spend time polishing them!

Why Do We Have Solos in the Church?

There is a historical tradition of singing solos in the church. The Old Testament is filled with poems and songs that told the story of the Hebrew children.

Then the prophet Miriam, Aaron's sister, took a tambourine in her hand; and all the women went out after her with tambourines and with dancing. And Miriam sang to them:
>"Sing to the LORD, for he has
>triumphed gloriously;
>horse and rider he has thrown
>into the sea."
>(Exod. 15:20-21)

Wow! An Old Testament soloist!

Church music traditions have taken many twists and turns in the years since Miriam sang her song. For many years, the song belonged to a soloist/composer, who then taught the people the song to sing. The song was the soloist's response to God's actions in his or her life. Since the time of Miriam, the tradition of who is to sing the song has moved back and forth between a choir, a soloist, and the congregation.

In the past ninety years, the tradition of solo singing has also twisted and made turns. For many years the song belonged to a trained choir or song leader, depending on your faith tradition and the community in which the church was situated. Around the turn of the century, the song moved from the people in the pew to the choir and soloists. We began to believe that only the trained professional singer had a song to offer. Voice teachers were making a living training persons to be church soloists. There were literally hundreds of sacred solos written and sung during the first fifty years of this century. It was the era of the "church soloist." I can remember a time when the biography in a concert program included a list of where the singer had been the "soloist," sometimes listing five or more local churches. Even today, if you look through the sacred music files of a large music store, you will find many solos with copyrights dating from this time.

Then came a change! In the 1960s, folk music began to come into the church. This was considered very radical, and many church musicians had to struggle with the "flower power" generation in music programs when the previous style of church music was considered the correct way of praising God. I remember the first time a friend and I sang a religious folk song with acoustic guitar accompaniment in a worship service. The tension was so thick you could have cut it with a knife! Looking back now, I am amazed that we were even allowed to sing this in the local church in which I was a member. The director of music truly stuck his neck out for us, and obviously kept it there as he continued to work with us and find ways for us to share in worship. (How the telephones must have buzzed with dire predictions of drums, electric guitars, and who knows what else to come next!) Technology in the 1980s brought solo accompaniment tapes into the church, many with difficult rhythms and vocal ranges, and a new stylistic term of "contemporary Christian music."

At the same time that tapes and CDs were being used in worship, the ancient tradition of the cantor was slowly being rediscovered. The cantor once again became the one to lead the song and to teach new songs.

What was happening in many local churches? Persons who

had been trained during the "church soloist era" were still continuing this tradition. Churches, pastors, and musicians began to question what was "good" church music and who was to perform it. In my new church position I learned that the leadership had not thought through the theology of sacred music in the church in quite a long time. Have you thought about your theology of church music lately?

God has given to each of us talents and gifts to use in God's service. Each person in the pew has been created to praise and worship the Lord, and each person has been given the gifts to do just that! Now, admittedly, in some folks the gift has been fine tuned and developed more than in others, but that doesn't negate the gift of the rest of the folks. It just means that we who have responsibility for musical leadership need to enable all persons to use their gifts to the best of their ability.

Why do we teach our children songs about the B-I-B-L-E, Jesus, and scripture phrases? So that they will learn to praise God and will be able to remember these new bits of information! Why was the story of the Christian people told in song? To praise God, to worship God, and to tell and teach the story of God and God's people. Recently, my district superintendent sang to me the books of the Old Testament, the New Testament, and the names of the twelve disciples all set to the tune "Twinkle, Twinkle, Little Star." Why did he take the time to do this? He recognized the need for persons to find a quick way to memorize these titles and names, and knew that by singing them they would be locked into the people's memories forever! People learn and are able to easily retell the story of God through song. The combination of music and word allows us to hear and feel the power of God's Word, and God's actions in our lives. Before the advent of the printing press, the availability of Bibles and hymnals, and a rising literacy rate, the sung song of God was one of the primary ways to tell the story of God and to be able to retell it over and over to others.

Putting all of this history stuff aside, in many churches, solos are the primary form of music leadership. Some churches have no organized choirs. Many music leaders have planned an occasional solo to allow the time for the choir to learn that really hard anthem—and let's not talk about those Sundays when everyone in the choir seems to have decided to go out of town! Solos sometimes seem to be a musical necessity in many church music ministry settings.

Another reality is that there are many "I am the bass soloist" personalities out there who need to be ministered to and listened to. While I encourage you to continue to work with those persons who have been singing solos, I hope to encourage and enable you to develop a whole new theology of solo church music leadership. This entire text will enable you to develop and create your own theology of music.

Who Is the Church Soloist?

Every member of your church music ministry has the potential to be a soloist! Honest! In order to make that a reality you will need to have a different understanding of the role of the soloist in worship. A soloist should serve as a musical leader of the worship service, and any other purpose will get in the way of that role. This means that the person who lines out a new hymn tune, the person who leads the antiphon to the psalm, and the person who sings the offertory are all serving as musical leadership, each serving as individual gifts and talents enable them. The church soloist can and should be every man, woman, and child who has chosen to serve God through music.

Your theology of church music will play an important role in the life of your church. What do you believe is the role of music in worship? Take the time to read and study several books on the subject; talk to other church musicians and clergy to get other views and opinions. Challenge yourself! *The*

Church Musician by Paul Westermeyer (Harper San Francisco, 1988), *Music and Worship in the Church* by Austin Lovelace and William Rice (Abingdon Press, 1960), and *The Church Music Handbook for Pastors and Musicians* (Abingdon Press, 1991) are places to begin your study and contemplation.

After your time of study, go back and take a very honest look at your "solo habits." Have you fallen into the trap of giving all of your solo works to the singer with whom you know you really don't have to spend very much rehearsal time? Have you used solos because of poor planning? Decide honestly if you need to make adjustments in your music ministry.

First, review the worship outlines and bulletins of your church. Where can music be used most effectively in your worship service? Are there places in the service where a sung response or act of worship may open the congregation to listen and hear God speak to them? Are there places in your worship where your congregation needs to be taught God's story so they can go out and retell it? Are there places where a single voice can be much more effective than a group of voices?

Next, look at who has chosen to serve God through participation in the music ministry. Does your choice of musical leadership reflect the makeup of those people? Do you only use adults as soloists and ignore youth and children (or the reverse)?

I have always encouraged all children to try out for a solo. I share with them that each song needs a special but different kind of voice to sing it—and they trust me to be fair. It is not unusual to have twenty of the thirty singers in my older elementary choir audition for a solo. They have even gotten pretty creative and supportive of one another and now create their own duet and trio groups to audition so that those who don't want to sing alone can have a chance. I have enough years of service in one church to see the results of this. Through this training, I have plenty of youth volunteering to serve as musical leaders. Some of my former children and youth choir members have grown up and are members of one of my adult choirs! They are still willing to serve as music leaders in worship.

My theology of church music is to seek and find the best that the Spirit of God has given to each member and help that person develop and train that gift so that it can be used to praise God! I have found that training each member to be a solo singer (to the best of his or her ability) is one way to live out this theology.

There are many books and resources to help you achieve this goal. This book is designed as a starting place. As you gain more skills and begin to create your personal theology of church music, continue to study and learn!

Chapter Two
Basic Vocal Techniques

I am one of those oddballs who actually spend their vacation Sundays visiting other churches. I have even been known to attend two or more services on one vacation day! I am also often dismayed to hear the untapped potential in a volunteer soloist. If only a few basics of vocal production had been shared I could have heard the voice raised to the best of the person's ability. The basics of vocal production are easily taught! Spend time practicing each of the basics and begin to learn to listen for the fullest potential in each person that you work with.

During my first semester of college, I remember watching my voice teacher during a master class session. She physically prepared for every note she sang. I could see her doing everything but producing the actual song! I honestly didn't understand what she was doing at that time, but now I find myself doing the exact same thing—and now I UNDERSTAND! The act of singing requires a total body and mind involvement. In this chapter, we will explore the physical experience of singing.

Throughout this chapter I will be giving you visual cues (or tricks of the trade) to use when working with the vocal soloist. I have found that using these cues makes vocal technique quickly understandable to persons of all ages and skill levels. They are also tools that the solo singer can use when practicing at home. Often, the best tool that you will have to use is your own body. Use your body to give the soloists a mirror image to copy. If you use good vocal technique the singer will copy it! If you are accustomed to hiding behind the keyboard, come out from behind it and practice breathing, standing, and stretching the musical phrase directly in front of the soloist so that he or she can see you clearly. Do not ask the soloist to do anything you are not willing to do. Practice these techniques so that you are comfortable with each of the concepts.

Also, remember that although I am giving you lots to work on in this chapter, do not throw all of this at your singers at one time. Just like the Sunday sermon, they can only remember a few primary points a week. You may use some of this (if not all, at some point) in your choir rehearsals and will only need to reinforce it when working one-on-one with your singers. Otherwise, decide which one or two skills are needed to be worked on this week and for the next several weeks emphasize these. Too much at one time is overwhelming and threatening, not to mention confusing. As one of my choir members said one week, "OK, you want us to sing the right pitches, rhythms, words, and dynamics, and now you want us to sing the whole thing musically too?" I realized that I had moved too fast in expectations for that rehearsal and reworked my lesson plans.

Use music the soloist is familiar with when teaching these skills. I constantly use the hymnal as a teaching tool; phrasing, vowels, consonants, and support can all be worked on using a familiar hymn. My choir member is right, choir directors are asking singers to remember a lot and all at one time. Why not make it easier, and more of a successful experience?

Also, keep in mind that your soloist needs to have time to get these vocal skills under control. Plan in advance so that singers do not have to jump from step one to step ten in just one or two weeks. These are progressively learned skills, so plan on giving singers the time they need to learn them. Later in this book, you will learn more about choosing the right repertoire to match skill level with each singer.

These truly are just the basics of vocal technique. Every voice needs to be listened to and treated as an individual instrument. If you begin to hear an instrument of great beauty emerging, I would suggest that you contact someone in your community who is professionally trained as a voice teacher and develop a relationship. A hardworking student with great potential is always welcomed by a voice teacher.

Posture

We have lost the art of standing up straight. We no longer practice walking with books on our heads as a part of deportment study. However, the very first step in singing is making sure that the instrument is in its best possible position to sing.

The importance of posture cannot be overemphasized. Posture is the foundation for the support needed to sing. The human voice is very much like any other wind instrument. It needs a clear passageway for the wind to enter and then move in a controlled manner over the vocal chords. Imagine a pipe from a pipe organ bent over in knots trying to speak the pitch (or picture a flute the same way).

Encourage the singer to use a music stand at first so that he or she can concentrate on body position. This will allow the singer to learn about what is good posture, without worrying about holding the music. Ask your soloists to stand with their body weight evenly distributed between their hips and feet. Many people stand with their weight on one leg with the other hip jutting up into the air—watch out for this! Your singers will probably need to be reminded to lift their rib cage. Women, especially, tend to roll their shoulders forward and to drop their rib cage. Often, simply asking the singers to roll their shoulders slowly up, around, and back to a rested position while lifting their rib cage at the same time will solve many posture problems.

Figure 1

Many times soloists get confused even with this concept, and so I ask them to picture a marionette singing. Ask your soloists to imagine that the marionette's strings are attached to their shoulders, breastbone, and the top of their heads. The puppeteer is pulling them straight up, lifting the rib cage, so that the head sits comfortably on top of the body. If a soloist tenses up and pulls his or her shoulders up out of alignment, ask the singer to imagine that the puppeteer has dropped the strings connected to the shoulders so the shoulders must drop also! Use the image of the marionette often during rehearsal, as old habits are hard to break and we all forget to hold good posture. This visual tool will help singers understand that sometimes you only need to realign one part of the body and everything else will naturally fall into place. It will also help them to visualize making an adjustment to only that one part without changing any other position. (See Fig. 1.)

Figure 2

Sometimes your singer will need a humorous character as a reminder about posture. Imagine yourself in the exaggerated posture of a grand opera tenor (complete with white handkerchief) or as Napoleon's wife Josephine in one of those frivolous dresses with stays and hoops. This image may seem ridiculous, but it gives an immediate mental and physical impression of good posture. (See Fig. 2.) These visual tools will enable the soloist to stand with good posture without getting terribly technical and threatening. After the singers become accustomed to these pictures you can switch to simply saying "Posture with ATTITUDE" and they will immediately straighten up to a good singing posture. Don't forget the old standby of asking your soloists to stand with their backs against a wall with their head, shoulders, hips, and heels touching the wall.

Keep your eye on your soloist and check his or her physical position while singing. Walk over to the person and make adjustments as needed to help him or her attain the best singing posture possible. It is fairly rare with untrained singers to have to make adjustments to the position that they hold their head. However, a few soloists will move their head as they sing up and down the scale. A gentle reminder that the puppeteer has control of their head and he has pulled the string up straight from the center of their head will eliminate this problem. Once again, a mirror will reinforce good habits if the singers can sing and watch themselves at the same time.

You and your singer will quickly discover that if you sing an entire solo using good posture (and adding the additional muscles used in supporting the sound) those muscles will tire out quickly. Your soloist will probably overdo everything you ask in the beginning, and will also become tired from nervous tension. You will need to remind your soloist to intentionally relax. I often work with the singer in planning a "relax" spot in the music and mark it accordingly. I use the phrase "drop and relax" in working with soloists. I have discovered that using a two-step concept helps both the soloist and the instructor to relax the muscles totally. Warn them that they may feel this muscular workout on the morning after your rehearsal until the muscles are strengthened.

One of the best teaching tools in vocal production is a mirror. Try to have a mirror in the room to help your soloists see what they look like when using correct posture. (See Fig. 3.)

Breath Control and Support

Let's start with the actual process of breathing first. In order to produce sound, pressurized air must pass over the vocal chords to cause them to vibrate. A singer needs to breathe in through the mouth quickly to get enough air into the lungs to sing the phrase. Then the singer must exhale that same air slowly. Most singers wait too long before inhaling

Figure 3

air and do not have time to prepare the body support needed to sing. Work with your singers in encouraging them to plan their breaths. Practice inhaling and exhaling over a variety of number of beats. It is sometimes helpful to practice slow inhalation through the nose. This is very relaxing and can help soothe nerves during a long introduction or interlude in the music. It is also pretty hard to mess up when breathing in slowly through the nose. As an example, breathe in through the nose during four pulses and exhale that same air over eight pulses on a controlled *s* (like a snake hissing).

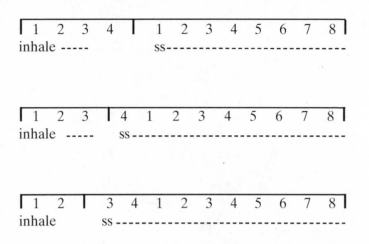

While breathing in through the nose feels great, it is not a luxury that we get often in singing. To make the transition, gradually shorten the number of inhale pulses and lengthen the exhale pulses. As you shorten the inhale pulse, your singer will need to begin to breathe in through the mouth in order to get enough air to last through the *s* section. At this point you need to do some anatomy lessons with the singer.

I find it ironic that we spend so much time teaching children the correct terms for everything these days and yet, we choir directors tell our singers to sing from the diaphragm and then rub our stomachs proudly. I once watched a friend in rehearsal discussing this subject, and I got a very unbecoming case of the giggles as I overheard one soprano say to the next, "but isn't a diaphragm a method of birth control?" Look at the diagram in Figure 4 and examine where the muscle connects and how it works. I believe that we must be very exact in teaching where and what the diaphragm is and what it does in relationship to the art of singing.

The diaphragm is a muscle that separates the upper chest organs (heart and lungs) from the lower part of the body.

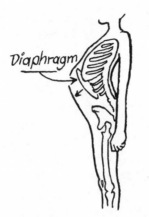

Figure 4

When we breathe in, the lower part of the lungs expands and the diaphragm drops and stretches down. In order to make room for the expansion of the lungs, the lower floating ribs are pushed outward and create a circle that stretches on all sides of your body, not just in the front. You should feel and see movement in the singer's back in this area as well. When the diaphragm stretches to the dropped position, the organs below the diaphragm are pushed down causing the abdomen to protrude slightly. The singer should not push out with the abdominal muscles—it will happen naturally. Notice that I haven't mentioned the upper chest or shoulders! Tell your singer that by maintaining correct posture, the shoulders and upper chest will not move when the singer inhales. (Easier said than done, I know!)

Using a slow nasal inhalation will help your singers to feel all of the motions of the stretching of their bodies as they breathe correctly. I often ask the singers to lie flat on their backs on the floor and to breathe very gently, gradually deepening their inhalation. They should then feel this stretching. Standing up, I then ask them to do the nasal inhalation exercise to a very slow pulse in this same position. Then I practice the same exercise but switch halfway through the nasal inhalation to breathing in through the mouth and nose, then I switch to inhaling totally through the mouth. This will take time and practice, and will take several weeks or longer to become a habit. Some singers will need to begin rehearsing on the floor for several weeks to overcome a lifetime of bad habits!

Then apply this same technique to the solo repertoire. When your soloist is comfortable with these breathing techniques start working with him or her in judging how much air is needed for varying lengths of phrases. Mark the music where the breaths are to be taken. The system that you use for marking is not important, but be consistent so the soloist will learn to know what the system is! My own system is this:

✔ : a breath

$\frac{1}{2}$
✔ : a short breath, usually just enough to get me to the end of the phrase without being concerned about making it to the end. I also use this occasionally for emphasizing the text.

?
✔ : an emergency breath, the place I can take a breath if needed to get me to the end of the phrase.

Planning these breaths can make for a much more musical performance and is also much less nerve-racking for the soloist!

In terms of inhalation, we know how to breathe and where to breathe. We have already worked a little bit on breath control in the inhalation exercise. Now we need to learn how to exhale all that air under control! We need to be intentional in understanding what is meant by breath control in exhalation. This involves controlling the diaphragm and the muscles around the rib cage and lower abdomen. Try saying "ha!" very loudly and quickly. Now, practice being a dying cowboy in your favorite western and try to exhale that same "ha" slowly, almost without a pitch—make it a really long and dramatic death! You have just controlled the amount of air passing over the vocal chords.

Now, I must say that controlling a singing tone while exhaling takes a little more effort, but it works on the same principle. The mistake most often made in breath control when singing is that we allow the chest, and often the whole body posture, to drop. Here's where I use visual aids to enable the soloist to picture the constant control needed for a singing phrase. Find a large, heavy-duty rubber band. Ask your singer to hold the rubber band between the thumb and forefinger of each hand. I prefer to position the hands so that one is touching the abdomen and the other is in front. Ask the singer to breathe in over an even pulse and then to sing the words of a familiar psalm on a single midrange pitch. Try this once, and then add a rubber band pull to the process. As the singer begins to sing, ask him or her to stretch the rubber band slowly and evenly between his or her hands throughout the sung phrase. This even, controlled, physical motion will enable them to maintain an even, controlled exhalation.

Initially, I allow the singer to drop the chest and shoulders and rest at the end of each text phrase. However, I quickly adjust the technique to continue the stretch throughout the next breath and next sung phrase without dropping the chest or posture. Once the soloist can do this comfortably, I ask him or her to breathe, set, and hold the support system without using the rubber band. This three-step process allows the singer to feel and judge each step of the way before singing. With more experience, this will happen almost simultaneously, but at first, take the time to allow the soloist to prepare the body to sing. With experience, your soloist will be able to sing an entire solo, never allowing the muscle to move without

being under control. The air will flow into the lungs and immediately turn and be exhaled under an even pressure.

Another cue that works much in the same way is pulling
taffy. Any slow, even, and controlled motion that does not
interfere with the breathing and posture process will work. I
have also used slow, full extension arm circles with success.
The arm rests down by the singer's side and when he or she
begins to sing, the singer slowly raises the arm in a full circle,
much like a windmill, matching the speed of the circle to the
length of the phrase and continuing into the next phrase without stopping.

Figure 5

Nowadays, every card shop has its own helium canister to
fill up balloons for a special day. The image of the helium canister is a great visual aid for singers. Imagine the canister as
your body after inhaling your breath. No matter how many
balloons are filled, the canister stays solid—it doesn't droop, or
tire out. It also lets out the helium to fill the balloon in a controlled manner. (See Fig. 5.) If you want to have a great choir
party, teach your choir all about support one week and end up
by filling and giving each person a helium balloon—they can't

miss the comparison. Of course, they'll all have to inhale some of the helium for that chipmunk voice effect, so plan on ending the choir rehearsal with a rousing version of the "Hallelujah!" chorus as a chipmunk choir!

Note this! Once your soloist/choir has begun to use these techniques, you might want to spend some time checking their vocal range. Altos and second sopranos are often reborn into lovely first sopranos when the support system is in place. Combine this support system with some basic techniques dealing with articulation and you may discover a second soprano has been hiding a beautiful high A or even higher! This also applies to the male voices in your choir.

Face and Mouth

Now, if you think your singers are going to laugh you out of the room when you ask them to support their sound like canisters of helium, just wait until you begin working on the face and mouth. Singers are incredibly self-conscious when you begin to work with their jaw, tongue, and mouth positions. All you have to do is to ask a singer to drop his tongue and it will feel like it has grown to a mammoth size in his mouth and it won't get out of the way no matter how hard he tries!

The first technique your singer will need to work on is simply opening her mouth. You will definitely need a mirror to prove that the singer is not dropping the jaw and opening the mouth. Ask the singer to stand in front of a mirror and to open her mouth. You may need to gently grasp her jaw and pull down on it to help her understand what you mean. If you have a china marking pencil you can draw the outline of her mouth when it is in the open position on the mirror, and then ask the soloist to match her mouth with the outline. Then use an exercise such as the one in Figure 6 to encourage her to drop her jaw to that point.

Figure 6

Zing - ah. _____

Note: Move to the "ng" as quickly as possible.

Move this up and down the scale in a comfortable range with your soloist. Then practice some of our hymn tunes that do the same, such as "Amazing Grace." If you practice this hymn with one pulse to the measure, each pulse can emphasize the dropped jaw. Ask your singers to drop their jaws on all of the vowels—even the long *e* of the word *me*. They won't like it and it will feel funny, but have them do it anyway. This will really work the dropped jaw technique for opening their mouths. Work on having them drop the jaw and leave it there for the full value of the note. Ask them to watch themselves in the mirror to see if they can catch themselves gradually closing their mouths. I have seen people use the three-finger-width technique to get singers to open their mouths, but the problem with that technique is that the fingers can be squashed together creating a smaller space, and besides, this rates about a 9.5 on the "looking stupid" factor. Also, you really can't sing and feel the space you have created by dropping your jaw, when there are multiple fingers crammed in your mouth. (I won't even get into the sanitation factor.)

If you don't teach your soloists and choir anything else in this section, this one technique, simply learning to drop the jaw, will improve the singing sound incredibly. This is also one place where your singer/choir will mirror you. If you are not opening your mouth when working with them, why should they do it for you? Keep your jaw loose and flexible. This tech-

nique, combined with support and posture, should create a
whole new sound for your singers. Tape them and let them
hear how much they have improved to this point; after all of
this hard work it's time for some positive reinforcement!

Vowels and Diphthongs

Have you ever noticed there is always one vowel that is
truly idiomatic to your area that really grates on your nerves?
In the Mechanicsville, Virginia area it is the *i* vowel. We will be
singing glorious vowel sounds, such as the cherubim in heaven
must use, when I see the word *ride* coming. It's only two measures away. I begin to sweat. I begin to overexaggerate a
dropped jaw, and then I hear a sound that seems as if someone
is pulling it through an eyeball. The closest I can come to
describing it to you is that it combines a bright *i* and *e* with a
little bit of dog howl mixed in. We constantly work on that
vowel, believe me. There are some sounds you will always
have to work on with your singers.

When working with a soloist's vowel sounds, you must listen to the voice as well as the vowel, and adjust the position of
the mouth to make the sound as beautiful as possible. When in
doubt, start with a dropped jaw—you can rarely go wrong
there. For example, we all know that the *ah* vowel needs to
have a dropped jaw, but as the singers move up the scale they
will need to drop the jaw even farther. Listen carefully to the
sound and work with the soloist in learning how much to drop
in order to create an even sound all the way up the range of the
solo. I usually close my eyes several times during this process so
that I can focus on the sound. Usually, this is where I begin, and
then I move on to some of the other sounds in the solo.

The worst vowel to work with, with most singers, is the *ee*
sound. We close our mouths when we speak this vowel and
simply do not want to open our mouths when singing it, and on

top of that it feels funny when we do! Sing an *ee* vowel up and down a scale dropping your jaw the higher you move up the scale. Besides being something we don't do naturally, this can even make your front teeth vibrate! Now, go back to the hymn "Amazing Grace" and sing it slowly, working on dropping your jaw, having the same sound throughout the hymn, feeling the placement of the vowels as you sing. You must feel this yourself before you can explain it to your soloist. When working on this technique, your singer will be amazed at the amount of sound he or she can produce! Tape this rehearsal session and let the singer hear the difference in the vowel sounds when the jaw is dropped.

A big voice will sometimes need a little more focusing to help control the sound, so just tell the singer to use fish lips! Yes, I know it sounds stupid, but imagine a big fish swimming along; his lips are thrust slightly forward and are opening and closing. Now try this with your vocalist. Some vocal teachers call this "point" or "cover," but fish lips works great with an untrained soloist. Ask the soloist to sing an *ah* and then tell him or her to add the fish lips. Listen to the sound, and adjust with more or less "lips" as needed to help focus the sound. Using a mirror to see what is happening throughout this process is almost necessary for the soloist to learn to feel and see this technique. (See Fig. 7.) Besides, your singers will definitely want to look at themselves on this one to make sure they really don't look stupid doing it!

Figure 7

Working on the vowels will often solve many intonation problems. This really does work hand in hand; the singer with pitch problems often doesn't open his or her mouth, and then hasn't really supported the sound, and so on.

Very occasionally, you will find a singer who is singing too "dark" sounding vowels, and this can also affect intonation. Our response is often to tell the singer not to drop the jaw so much, but I have a much better solution. This also will help persons who are slightly out of tune or too tired physically to support the sound to keep it in tune. Imagine a face, now place a large butterfly on the face. The body of the butterfly is in line with your nose, the large top portion of its wings stretches out and across your cheekbones, and the remainder of the wings stretch down on either side of your mouth as it is opened in a beautiful dropped jaw *ah.* Now, gently, ever so gently, imagine the upper wings lifting the muscles across your cheeks up and back into your temples. While you continue to drop your jaw this lifting motion adds a brilliance to the sound without changing the basic position. This brilliance will often lift the pitch right into place. (See Fig. 8.)

Figure 8

The diphthong is a dirty word in a singer's vocabulary. What are diphthongs? Go back to "Amazing Grace" and hold onto the second syllable of the word *amazing.* You will need to sing not only the *eh* sound but also the *ee* sound to create the syllable. (Try to sing "say," "sure," and "round," and listen for the diphthong.) You always want to sing the primary vowel for the longest time possible and then throw in the secondary sound at the absolute last second. If the singer is holding a dropped jaw position for the full value of the note, it's really hard to get that diphthong in there! So emphasize holding the dropped jaw position rather than going into a long discussion about the diphthong. Diphthongs are all around us waiting to take over our singing. Keep an ear open for them, listen for the primary vowel sound, and hang onto it for dear life!

Consonants

So where do we go now? Consonants! After all, without consonants we don't have the rest of the word. Ask your soloists to say the text of the piece out loud. Can you understand the text? If they cannot say it clearly, they will not sing it clearly. Work with singers in discovering which consonants they will need to emphasize. Now try to sing the piece. Some consonants are sung, which means you can hold a pitch while singing them (*m, n, ng, b, d*), while some consonants are not sung (*k, p, t, f, h, s*). Use the sung (or "voiced") consonants to enhance *legato* singing and to work on continuing that *legato* through the unsung (or "unvoiced") consonants. Consonants such as *p* are called explosive consonants and must have a minuscule silence afterwards in order to be understood. Others, such as *f,* use an air sound as part of the consonant and that must be planned into the rhythmic timing. Speaking the text will alert you and the soloist to any potential problems. Watch how the text is printed in the music! Music publishers follow the rules for separating words for singing, but that may not visually help the singer. Recently, I received an anthem that had the word *scorching* separated as "scorch - ing." I immediately noted that as a trouble spot and instructed the singers to mark the word in their scores as "sco - rching" to remind them of what it should sound like. Look for these and alert your singer to them.

One of my personal pet peeves is understanding the distinction between *t* and *d*. I have listened to many soloists singing praises to their "Lort and Got"! Say the word *cat* slowly. Feel where the *t* lies. Now, say the word *dog* slowly. Feel where the *d* lies. Move back and forth between the two consonants. Use this simple exercise whenever there is any question as to which consonant is which!

There are as many vocal techniques available in the world as there are voices. Keep trying a variety of ways to enable your singers to understand, feel, and do the technique you want them to work on. Constantly be looking for new ways to say and show these vocal techniques. Each person learns in a slightly different way. Keep trying until you find the way that works best for you and your solo singers!

Chapter Three
Choosing Repertoire

Carole has a beautiful tenor voice and is blessed with a very good ear. He only needed to hear his part once or twice and then he was able to hold the tenor part against the rest of the choral parts. It is rare for him to miss rehearsal or a worship service. He regularly tells me that he can't read music (which to him means he doesn't know the names of the notes) but that he has learned to see if the notes went up or down and if they were long notes or fast ones— "the ones that are big circles versus the ones that have those little flags on them." He is willing to sing a solo if I work with him. Once the date for his solo is set, however, this very secure choir member turns into a very nervous soloist! We worked together and discovered some little tricks to help him. For instance, he discovered that he was most comfortable when he used a music stand to hold the music, and he never sang without a small writing pen in one hand that he could squeeze to help get rid of extra nervous energy.

Using the terminology "inexperienced soloist" does not imply that the singer is not a good singer, but the pressures of singing alone versus singing in a choir or even in a duet can change your potential soloist into a creature you have never met before! When choosing repertoire for the inexperienced, reluctant, or even the experienced soloist, there are several guidelines that you should consider following. I use many of these guidelines when choosing repertoire for myself! My choice of the music for the solo is part of my ministry of caring for the soloist, part of my response to my call as a director of music ministry.

Practical Matters: Voice Type, Vocal Range, Musical Skill Levels

All sopranos are not created equal. This can be said of other voice parts as well. You must work with your soloist to find out exactly what is the range of his or her voice. Just because someone tells you that he or she is a soprano or a tenor does not mean that the person can sing a solo range of a soprano or tenor. Singing in a particular section in the local church choir also can mean that the individual came in and sat next to a good friend who just happened to sing soprano or tenor. It may also mean that this was the part the "soprano" could sing when she was younger but no one has worked with her enough to discover that she can no longer sing a soprano range. Or it may mean that the "tenor" could read music and a music reader was really needed on the tenor part and the singer never moved back to his own voice part!

You will need to check the vocal range of your singers. I suggest that you consider checking the range of all of your singers soon after they join a choir and then again every couple of years. We all have heard the various scale patterns that are used in some settings, but this is very threatening to someone who is not really sure about doing this "solo stuff." You are also not looking for the absolute top and bottom of the vocal range, you are looking for the comfortable range. You do not want to use the absolute top or bottom of an inexperienced soloist's range. It is rarely a pretty sound when a nervous soloist is heading toward a pitch he or she can only reach singing "ah" on a scale and a prayer! I use familiar hymns that have a wide range to check the comfortable vocal range.

Some of these hymns include:

UMH No.	Title	Range/Notes
378	"Amazing Grace"	Octave: C-C, well-known tune
145	"Morning Has Broken"	9th: C-D, use the first line only
213	"Lift Up Your Heads"	Octave: D-D, for those who prefer a scale pattern
217	"Away in a Manger"	Octave: C-C, use this with caution, practice learning to use good support to begin singing at the top of the phrase.

(Note: UMH refers to *The United Methodist Hymnal*.)

Modulating up a half step between verses or phrases will allow you to judge the comfortable top range of your soloist. Moving down in the same manner will let you judge the bottom range. This tune should be so well known that your singer will be able to overcome any nervousness in singing for you very quickly. This will not give you the true vocal range of your soloist, but I believe the information of the "comfortable range" is more important, especially when working with an inexperienced soloist.

Next, listen to your singer carefully to consider the natural voice quality. Toaster settings and voice qualities have much in common—they range from very light to very dark. (See Fig. 9.)

You must listen to the voice, not the song, to discover the voice quality and you will need to develop a consistent system for classification. The terminology that you choose is not as important as the consistency of the system. Voices are called light or dark, are described in terms of colors (bright white to dark blue), and are placed within a range of vocal classifications such as lyric or dramatic. Many of you may be surprised to learn that a prima donna is not a voice quality, but a personality type!

Figure 9

Many choral singers have learned to adjust their vocal sound for a specific musical style. I usually ask the singer to sing a variety of hymn styles to help me discern the vocal quality. Recently, a colleague who had only heard me sing in a light lyric sound in my work with children's choirs, happened to attend a concert of opera selections in which I was performing *Aida*. I am a dramatic soprano, but I am able to adjust my sound as is appropriate to the musical style and setting. Your singer will learn to do this, but it will not be something he or she is comfortable doing in the beginning of his or her solo experience.

The Myers-Briggs Personality Preference Indicator is a tool many persons use to find out what their personality preferences are. This does not mean that they are not able to use other qualities of their personality, just that these qualities are the personality preference. Every voice has a personality preference too.

You will need to discover what the voice naturally wants to do. Some voices want to sing long phrases and slow, sustained passages. These voices can sing an *adagio* phrase with no difficulty and can hold on to a long stretched musical phrase forever. They have difficulty singing a phrase that contains long and quick runs or one that uses a pattern of rapid, rhythmic leaps of intervals of a third or larger. On the other hand, a voice that wants to move literally quivers with frustration on long, slow phrases and moves with ease and joy on runs or rhythmic leaps. Most voices are somewhere in the middle.

Once again, I suggest that you use hymn tune phrases to assist you in judging the voice preference.

UMH No.	Title	Notes/Purpose
288	"Angels We Have Heard on High"	Ability to move quickly; use the first phrase of the refrain only, repeating and accelerating each time
502	"Thy Holy Wings, O Savior"	Ability to move quickly; sing through the verse, accelerating throughout
108	"God Hath Spoken by the Prophets"	See notes on No. 502
221	"In the Bleak Midwinter"	Ability to hold a slow *legato;* hold each note for full value, sing at a moderately slow tempo
171	"There's Something About That Name"	See notes on No. 221
521	"I Want Jesus to Walk with Me"	See notes on No. 221

It is obvious that a music reader will usually learn a solo faster than a nonreader. However, the ability to retain a melody line is a gift that reaches beyond the distinction between reader and nonreader. A nonmusic reader with a high level of melody retention will probably be able to sing with confidence a slightly more difficult melody line than a music reader with a low level of melody retention.

There is one more judgment that you will need to make concerning the musical skill level of the soloist. Take an honest look at the musical style and basic vocal skill capabilities that the soloist can perform. You will also need to remember that what your singer can do in a choral group setting is not necessarily what he or she can do in a solo setting.

I have never sung in a professional solo performance as well as I personally wanted to perform. I can always hear something I could have done better. Listening to a recording after the performance, I have looked at the person listening with me and said, "There! Did you hear that?" They usually look at me as if I were crazy because they are not listening for the same fine nuances of voice, musical phrase, or style that I felt were needed. What got in the way of my performance? The same things that may get in the way of your inexperienced soloist's performance. Nerves are known to hit musicians at the strangest times. I am often nervous for what I think is absolutely no reason and every singer reacts to nerves in a different way. Some singers speed up the tempo, some slow it down, some grab for air on every word, some forget to sing! Many soloists have been known to blank out and begin to concentrate on who is in the congregation rather than on what they are singing. The inexperienced soloist will often forget all of those wonderful musical phrases you worked on, and simply pray that he or she can get through this experience and just SIT DOWN! This is why it is so important to choose repertoire carefully for the inexperienced soloist. I would rather err on the side of the "too easy" piece of music and know that the experience was good for all involved—the soloist, the director, and the congregation—than to burden the soloist with a difficult piece before he or she is adequately prepared to sing it.

Which comes first: the chicken or the egg? Which comes first: the choice of the solo work or the soloist? Your local church setting, soloists, and worship styles may lean towards one answer or another. No matter what the answer, you will need to make some decisions concerning the voice type, range, quality, vocal personality type, and musical skill level of the soloist as well as making the exact same decisions about the vocal needs of the actual solo work.

Start a record system on your soloists. Using an index card, a notebook, or a computer data base, keep track of your soloist information including range, voice quality, and so on. Make adjustments as your singer gains experience. You will discover that the comfortable singing range will widen, the voice will become more flexible, and the self-confidence level will soar! Use this record system to keep track of what solos your singer sings, how often, and any other pertinent information you'd like to include.

If you have a need for solos on a regular basis, you may want to start a cross-referenced file of the solo work vocal requirements also. An index card cross-reference file, or even making notes on the top of the printed music will work as well. Use whatever system will fit your needs the best. If you use the hymnal as a resource for solo singing, make notes in your copy about the arrangement you used or created as well as the range and any other pertinent information you have.

Now that you have decided the musical requirements, you must also consider the criteria for choosing a text!

Text Concerns

More and more local churches are discovering the lectionary. The lectionary is a three-year cycle of biblical texts that incorporates an Old Testament lesson, psalm, Epistle lesson, and Gospel lesson. The Sunday lessons are listed using the Christian year and each of the three years are labeled A, B, or C. I have added this information to my record-keeping system, even though not all of the clergy I have worked with have used the lectionary. Why? I still can use lectionary resources to help me in deciding on music for a worship service. Although the pastor's choice of text for the second week in February may actually appear in the lectionary on the thirteenth Sunday after Pentecost, the lectionary resources are still usable. I have discovered that more often than not, the scripture lesson appears somewhere in the three-year cycle of the lectionary. Although your clergyperson may not be using the lectionary, you can use lectionary resources to give you ideas about what hymns, anthems, or solos are appropriate for that scripture lesson.

There are also several books available that list suggested solos by the scripture. Most of them were created and printed as a part of a doctoral thesis. I have found each resource to be slightly different according to the musical style preference of the editor, so I have collected several in order to have a wide variety of choices. Most of these collections are printed by a small local publishing company or the authors themselves. If you see one in a store, grab it right then! You may never see another one again. I have listed two sources I have used in the bibliography.

Another issue that you will need to consider is inclusive language. Once again, I use my card system to note inclusive language concerns. I will not use this forum to discuss the inclusive language issue, but whether or not it is a concern for you at this time, it may become a concern as your church, clergy, or personal opinion on this issue changes. Why not start your card system off with all the information you may need, either now or in the future?

Do you know what translation of the Bible is used in your local church? What translation do you give to children, youth, or adults as gifts from your church? Very few churches are concerned about which biblical translation is reflected in the solo text. However, if you have chosen to use the solo as the scripture lesson reading, there may be enough difference in the text because of translation to affect the sermon or the response to the Word.

If you choose a solo text that is in a language not spoken fluently by the members of your congregation, you will need to make the decision about what language in which to sing the text. Your decision as to the language issue will need to be made depending on the tradition and custom of your local church and the language skill level of your soloist. If you choose to sing in a language that is foreign to your congregation there are several options available to translate the text.

1. Print the translation in the bulletin.
2. Read the translation prior to the musical act of worship.
3. Sing the translation as part of the musical act of worship. For example, if you have chosen "¡Canta, Debora, Canta!" (UMH No. 81) as a solo, you can sing the text in Spanish as well as in English.

There are literally thousands of solo texts to choose from that are not literal translations of scripture. There are many beautiful texts that are wonderful expressions of faith and witness, and then there are those that are not! Here are some questions and issues that you will need to answer when choosing a nonscripture text.

• Will the text stand alone without the music? Often musicians get so wrapped up in the beauty of the music that they forget to really study the text. Read the text as a poem or story. Is this text still something you want to use in your worship service?

- What does this text say about God and our relationship with God? Music is used as an act of worship—is this text something you want to lift up as an offering to God? It is sometimes difficult to distinguish a sacred text from a secular love song. Truly take time to prayerfully consider what this text says. Consider also where the work will be used in worship. Does this text reflect the movement of the Spirit where you have chosen to use the solo?

- Does this text reflect the doctrines and theology of the church in which you serve? For some this is not an issue; for me it is a significant issue. I have chosen to serve in a local congregation of The United Methodist Church, and that choice impels me to reflect the theology and doctrines of the church. If you have not studied the doctrine and theology of the church where you are serving, there are several resource materials available. Every denomination has published their doctrines and theological statements. Ask your pastor if you can borrow your denomination's resources on this subject.

- For what season or special day in your church worship is this text most appropriate? Remember the lectionary? A cross-reference of the lectionary themes will help you decide what season or day to use this text. To reverse the process, using a Bible commentary to help you explore the scripture lesson for the day may help you see the potential use for a nonscripture text.

- Finally, you must decide if this text is appropriate for your local church setting. Does the poetic style in which it was written match the needs of your church or is it too stilted, romantic, or contemporary? If this is a concern, consider what you can do to enable the text to be used. I have written a commentary or explanation of the text to be printed in the bulletin for some texts. This is especially helpful if the text is a characterization of a personal story. If the soloist is singing a shepherd's prayer written by an eighteenth-century English writer, a note about this in the bulletin will help your congregation understand the role this solo serves in the worship service.

Why are these text considerations important to the inexperienced soloist? Beyond all of the issues discussed earlier, an inexperienced soloist will need to feel comfortable with the text in order to feel as if his or her offering during the service is adding to, and not subtracting from, the worship service. Actually, we all should be conscious of this, inexperienced and experienced soloists alike!

Choosing repertoire for the inexperienced soloist takes time and study and there are many questions that you will need to answer. The choice of the repertoire is one of the most critical factors in the development of your soloist. Your soloists need to know that the music is within their capabilities, that the text is a text they can believe in, and that the solo will be an offering worthy of lifting in praise to God. They will also need to feel good enough about what they have done to want to learn more about singing and to want to have more opportunities to sing a solo.

Chapter Four
What Does a Printed Solo
Have that You Don't Have?

D o you sometimes feel like a mystical Swami, who is supposed to know the answer before anyone even asks the question? I have felt that way more than once. A member of your choir has finally agreed to sing a solo. HAL-LELUJAH! His parting shot out of the choir room is "You go ahead and pick the song, just don't make it too hard, and I really like that song that I heard on the radio the other day. The title? No, I don't remember. The name of the artist or any of the words in the song? Well, no I didn't get that either, but boy, I sure liked it—find one just like it for me, OK?" What do you do?

Most of us would run to a music store and dig through a pile of music, hoping to find the perfect solo for the singer. One day while trying to stand back up after digging through the bottom drawer of a file cabinet of solo music, I decided that I had had enough! (Have you ever noticed that the sacred solos are always in the very bottom drawer of the cabinet?) I was looking for a printed solo that included a simple melody, an interesting accompaniment that doubled the voice part, in a medium range. When you factor in the cost of two copies of solo sheet music or collections, my frustration level was reaching the absolute limit. Another reality is that publishers do not publish a wide variety of vocal solo sheet music.

I couldn't find published solos that fit my need for my reluctant soloist. I believe we church musicians need to learn how to create our own solo arrangements out of self-defense!

Use Your Hymnal!

The obvious answer had been in my hands the whole time! Several of the hymns in the hymnal are "ready-to-wear" solos. They have an interesting accompaniment and can easily be sung "as is." For example, "Spirit Song" (UMH No. 347) can be sung as it is printed in the hymnal, since the accompaniment is interesting and supports the singer by doubling the melody. Many hymns are intended to be sung in unison and make great solos! Look through your hymnal for these hymns and mark them as potential solos. "Cantemos al Señor" (UMH No. 149) is another example of a "ready-to-wear" solo. Although it has a wide range, it only touches the bottom of the singer's range and does not go above D. The vowel sound on the D is an open "ah." It could be used in a wide variety of ways in worship: as a Call to Worship, an Act of Praise, a Response to the Word, a Response to a Baptism, a hymn with the congregation singing the refrain, or the Psalm of the Day (Psalm 19). This is a very flexible "hymn solo." It would work well with all ages of soloists. Depending on what your tradition is in your local church you could use guitar or piano accompaniment, adding Hispanic rhythm patterns with percussion instruments if you and your soloist would like to do so.

The United Methodist Book of Worship also has several solo possibilities in it. Works such as "Doxology" (BOW, No. 182) by Steve Garnaas-Holmes and "Come, Be Baptized" by Gary Alan Smith (BOW, No. 173) can be used "as is" when used as a response in worship. There will be more information about these in the next chapter.

The rest of the hymnal is waiting for you to use as a solo!

In order to make hymns into solos you will need to be creative. Although you can use the four-part harmonization of the hymn as the accompaniment for your singer, most singers need to feel that their solo will offer something a little different. So what do you do?

Some keyboard players have been truly blessed and are able to make up a wonderful accompaniment pattern to a solo without even thinking about it; others of us have to work at it! If you want to create your own accompaniment, take a few minutes to analyze the harmonization. Many of our hymns have fairly simple chord progressions and you can use basic chord accompaniment patterns to create an interesting accompaniment. If you can't remember the chord progressions write them into your hymnal and then play around with a variety of accompaniment patterns until you have several that you feel comfortable with. Depending on your interpretation of the text and the number of verses you will be using, you may want to change your patterns during the solo. Just be sure to decide in advance the patterns you will use and when you will play them so that your soloist will be comfortable with the accompaniment patterns.

Some of the most important elements of a solo you will need to prepare for, in advance of your rehearsal, are the introduction, interludes, or bridges between verses, and the ending or coda. These are some of the things that a printed solo has that we often don't consider when planning on using the hymnal as a solo resource. Remember, you must plan these out and have them set before working with your singer. Your soloist will need to feel secure about when to begin to sing and if you change the introduction or interlude at each rehearsal your soloist will not feel good about the experience of singing a solo.

When deciding on the introduction to the solo consider the capabilities of your soloists. Will they need to hear a portion of the melody before they sing? Do they need to hear the last few measures of the hymn to know when to come in? The answers to these questions will help you decide on the introduction. Interludes will allow the soloist to rest and also serve to lead us into the mood of the next verse.

Consider the text of the hymn. Do you need to make a transition from a flowery verse to a strong verse? Or the reverse? Work at altering your accompaniment style to match or create the mood change. Consider not playing any portion of the melody and using the chord progression only. Practice and make sure that your soloist can retain his or her tonal center if you decide not to use any portion of the melody in the interlude. Sometimes not using an interlude is an effective tool to enhance musical phrasing and style, especially if the thought and mood of the verse text is continued from one verse to the next.

Alter your accompaniment patterns as you feel necessary to uplift and undergird the text. Refer to any piano chord playing course for a refresher lesson and ideas on how to use block, arpeggio, Alberti bass, and other accompaniment patterns. Also, remember to consider moving the accompaniment an octave higher or lower, in either hand or both hands for variety. You may want to consider using the alto or tenor line, played up an octave, as a descant in the accompaniment. If you have the "gift" of transposition, modulate or transpose the hymn to add interest. If you don't have the gift, collect a variety of denominational and nondenominational hymnbooks. Many hymn tunes appear in different keys in other hymnals. Some denominations also print selected hymns in lower keys as separate books. Ask!

The grand finale! You can undoubtedly improve upon those printed sheet music endings and codas. Depending on the text, ask your singer to try retarding the final phrase of the hymn or repeating the last phrase or chorus. Use one of your interludes to lead into the last phrase or you may want to add a coda played by the keyboard.

If you are using the organ as the accompanying instrument, you have an even wider range of options available to you to use. Use creative registrations to accompany your soloist! I collect every hymn harmonization collection that I can find. These make great additions to the "create your own" solo repertoire. Use alternate harmonizations to offer a variety of accompaniments or to offer a modulation and harmonization. Watch carefully that the solo is not modulated out of the vocal range of the soloist and that the soloist can sing the melody line against the harmonization. Also, many organ harmonizations can be used on piano with a minimum of adjustment.

One word of caution! This is really fun to do and we musicians can go a little overboard and create incredible monstrosities called accompaniments. Be sensitive to the needs of your soloist at all times. The accompaniment should support the singer, not overwhelm the singer.

The Music and Worship Planner, written by David Bone and Mary Scifres and published annually by Abingdon Press, suggests a hymn arrangement for each week for use by the choir. I have used this idea as a starting place for solo arrangements as well. Often their suggestions work to create a solo without any adjustments. Sometimes you will only need to make a few adjustments to work around choir versus solo issues.

The options for creating your own solo arrangements are endless. It is like going to a great buffet dinner where all of your favorite foods are prepared—you get to pick and choose!

Octavos and Choral Collections

For some reason, we directors rarely consider using choral music as a potential solo. I suggest that you start a new file of anthems that can be used as solos. Not every octavo can be used, but with thought and preparation many can become wonderful solos.

Play and sing through your children's choir repertoire or any unison anthems you have in your music library. Some of these texts are not appropriate for an adult singer, but on the other hand, many children's anthems take on a new life when sung by an adult soloist. An adult's faith journey and experience can add a special text emphasis that you had never considered when working with children. "Prayer for Today" by Margaret Tucker, published by Choristers Guild, is arranged as a children's choir anthem, but an adult brings such a different interpretation to this text that is equally as valid and beautiful. One warning! You may have to work around the cover art of some children's anthems. One of my soloists was insulted that I had given her a "kid's" solo to sing because it had a cover filled with cute little sheep on the front. Once she worked on the piece and understood what she could bring to the work, she was thrilled to be able to interpret this Bible text in such a special way. This work, written by John Horman and published by Choristers Guild, is entitled "The Lost Sheep." An adult shepherd tells the story from a different point of view than a child shepherd and this work makes the transition beautifully.

When considering using an anthem that was written for multiple voice parts as a solo work, you have several things to consider. First you must decide if the melody will stand alone as a solo musical line without the full choral sound. Not all melody lines will! Try singing through the entire work, singing only the melody line. You probably just discovered more of those issues that you will need to resolve before choosing an octavo as a solo.

An anthem setting may modulate several times and the melody may switch from women's voices to men's voices.

Sometimes it is very difficult for a soloist to find the melody when it switches between the clefs. This is one time when being a nonmusic reader is an advantage. I have found that this is not an issue with most nonreaders, who just need you to get them started and they will sing the melody line.

What is the range of the melody? Does the clef switch and the modulations create an uncomfortable range for the soloist? One trick I have used is to pull one copy of the octavo to be used as the soloist copy and highlight in bright yellow the melody line and text throughout the work.

Carefully consider the text, especially if the melody line moves between the women's and men's voices. You may need to adjust some pronouns to match the gender of the soloist. If the text refers to "son" and a woman is singing it, this may cause some confusion. Double check all gender-specific terms. Write the adjustment in parentheses above the text line in advance to save rehearsal time and confusion.

Finally, consider the accompaniment. Will this accompaniment work if only the melody line is being sung or do you need to add some notes to fill out the harmonization of the accompaniment? Are there places where you will need to play countermelodies that appear in the other choral parts? Is the accompaniment written to support a SATB choir too full to be used as a solo accompaniment? You will also need to adjust your accompanying style and volume. What has worked for a full choral sound will probably not work as a solo accompaniment. Adjust organ registration as appropriate for your soloist. If you can, pull a copy of the music to be kept as the solo accompaniment edition and mark your copy as needed.

Many denominations have published collections of accompaniments for choirs to be able to sing hymns right out of the hymnal as anthems. What are you waiting for? Use these as arrangements for soloists as well!

Keyboard Music

Now, reverse your thinking process and consider going to your keyboard music files first! Many organ or piano solo arrangements can be used as "ready-to-wear" solo accompaniments. Pull out your collections of hymn tune keyboard solos and chorale preludes!

You will need to judge the usability of the keyboard work as the accompaniment for a vocal solo. Look at and sing through the range of the melody line throughout the work. Is it still within the comfortable singing range of your soloist? Will this work if your soloist needs to sing the melody an octave lower or higher than it is played? Where does the melody appear? A melody line in the pedal is rather difficult to sing to! Will your soloist be able to hold the melody line steady against the harmonization? Will the soloist know when to begin singing or does the arrangement use too small fragments of the hymn tune interspersed with other music to work as a vocal solo? Is the original work too "big" sounding to sing against? These are important questions that you will need to answer about each keyboard work that you are considering for use as a vocal solo arrangement.

Even if the total work does not meet the criteria to be used as is, rethink the possibility for use as introduction, interlude, or ending. Use the solo organ or piano work hand in hand with your hymnal. One of my own solo arrangements was created out of a moment of desperation. I was asked to sing for a wedding with a large wedding party and what seemed like a thousand sets of parents and grandparents. With today's changing society, it is not unheard of to have eight sets of grandparents! The organist for the wedding was dreading playing an eternal recessional and asked me to try to come up with "something, anything, HELP!" My solution was to use Paul Manz's organ solo arrangement of "God of Grace and God of Glory," published by Concordia. The organ solo incorporates the melody line with a very festive sounding interlude. We transposed the hymn to the same key as in Mr. Manz's arrangement and created a recessional/solo that incorporated the traditional hymn setting and Mr. Manz's organ solo setting. I sang several verses as arranged by Mr. Mantz and the congregation sang a verse out of the hymnal. The entire wedding party got out of the church without the rest of us being bored to tears!

Finally, I encourage you to try your hand at composing solos that will fit your soloists and worship services to a T. It is becoming easier today to use computers with MIDI (Musical Instrument Digital Interface) resources to compose at the keyboard and have the music printed immediately. Many colleges are now offering courses in composition. Why not stretch your wings and see what God has in store for you?

What does printed music have that you don't have? While a printed solo may have the composer's interpretation of the text, it may not fit your needs. You can create your own solos to fit the precise needs of your "reluctant soloist" with a little time and effort. You can minister to your soloists by matching their own needs and skills with solos that will serve as acts of worship and fulfill the faith community's need to share talents and gifts in worship.

Chapter Five
Not Everyone Is Ready for the Big Time

Hidden in your choir is a potential soloist. Honest! There is a diamond in the rough sitting in your choir loft! He is probably at choir rehearsal every week and you've never really heard his voice all alone. Except maybe that one Sunday when he was the only member of the tenor section who showed up to sing and, well, admit it, you were kind of surprised at how much potential you heard in his voice.

Then there was the week when you were leading the alto section in sectionals and you thought you heard a really nice sound out of someone that you had never really heard before.

So what do you do now?

You will need to be sensitive, supportive, and patient when working with a member of your choir who has never considered himself or herself a soloist. This needs to be a very positive experience or you will never get that person back up for a solo.

Do not ask the choir member to sing the solo while in front of other people! Wait until you have a moment alone with your singer and tell him or her honestly that you have heard great potential in his or her voice. Share with the singer some key points:

    1. You have in mind an act of worship that would be perfect for his voice type.

2. You would very much like to help her develop her full potential as a singer.
3. You will be there for him and help him every step of the way.
4. You understand her fears and will do everything to help her overcome them.

Show your soloist-to-be the music you have in mind for her and explain how it will fit in worship. If she seems hesitant, ask her to pray about it—and you pray too!

All of the criteria listed in chapters 2 and 3 still need to be considered. No matter how short the solo, be it four measures or four hundred measures, it is your ministry to the soloists in your choir to choose the repertoire wisely, to prepare them to the best of their ability, and to enable them to share their gifts and talents in praise to God.

Now what kinds of repertoire do you choose for the first time soloist? There are many solos that are perfect for the "first timer" in your choir loft. You will need to adjust your understanding of what role a solo can play in worship. Remember how you considered your theology of church music in the first chapter. Your first timer can become a song leader for a hymn or a cantor for the psalm. Look for opportunities for solos other than as the major musical focus for the day, such as the typical offertory solo seems to be in most churches. In addition to lessening the pressure on your soloist, this will help him or her understand the role of music in worship beyond the offertory or anthem "slot."

• The first timer as cantor: What is a cantor? The word *cantor* is a term for someone who leads the congregation in music as an act of worship. For example, use your first time soloist to sing the antiphon through one time before the congregation joins in. No one ever died from singing solo for six to eight measures!

• The first timer as teacher: Isn't it time for the congregation to learn a new hymn? Ask your soloist to sing the first verse as a solo to help teach the hymn to the congregation. If you have the tradition of teaching a new hymn during the gathering time, your soloist can help there as well. Even if you have decided to sing a familiar hymn, having a soloist sing one verse can add a new dimension to your congregational music. At the close of Palm/Passion Sunday worship consider using "Ah, Holy Jesus" (UMH No. 289) as the closing hymn. A soloist could sing verse 2 to emphasize the personal meaning of the text. Use your bulletin to announce any changes to the "norm" of hymn singing for your congregation!

For example:

UMH No. 289 "Ah, Holy Jesus"   HERZLIEBSTER JESU
Congregation: Verse 1
Soloist: Verse 2
Congregation: Verses 3-5

Hymns that are written in the call and the response model are great opportunities for solos. "O Mary, Don't You Weep" (UMH No. 134) is perfect for the first time soloist. The range is very limited, the tune is familiar, and each verse is only four measures long! Other hymns to consider are hymns that have a refrain. The soloist can sing the verse and the congregation can respond by singing the refrain. Different soloists could sing the verses. Look in the index of your hymnal for hymns that could serve as service music. Often a short hymn solo or refrain is the perfect response to prayer, to the scripture, and so on.

The United Methodist Book of Worship includes a section entitled "Music as Acts of Worship." These are new to United Methodists and are designed for congregational singing. Many make wonderful solos. Use these as solos for a week or two before asking the congregation to sing them.

Be creative in finding solos within your Sunday anthem. Even though the anthem says all sopranos, make it a solo! Many anthems have at least a small section that is in unison— consider this as a possible solo, being conscious of the range and text.

Is your soloist-to-be a soprano or a tenor? Pull out the descant to your hymnal and ask him or her to sing a descant as a solo on the last verse of a congregational hymn. It is a solo without the soloist having to sing alone! Look for pieces of music that call for a single voice part to sing over an ostinato (such as in the style of Taizé).

Do you have several first timers spread throughout your choir? Why not adapt an anthem to a duet or trio or quartet? Even a small section of your regular Sunday anthem can be sung by these first timers!

One last idea! Are you playing a prelude or offertory based on a hymn tune? Ask your first timer to sing a verse of the hymn prior to the playing of the prelude or offertory.

Chapter Six
Preach It!

As a private music instructor, several of my students have gone on to vocal competitions. Preparing for a competition is very different from preparing for singing in church and yet in some ways they are very similar. As I teach pieces that may be used in competition, I will often ask, "That's perfect for the competition, now would you perform differently when singing this for a concert or as part of a worship service?" The difference is in how the singer approaches the telling of the story. While I still have the same expectations of vocal technique and musical phrasing, if the solo is to be used in worship it needs to be a vital connected part of worship. As we Southerners say, "That'll preach!"

What Does the Text Mean?

Have you thought about the text you are asking your soloist to sing? What does the text say to you? Can you relate to it in any way? Spend time reading the text silently or out loud to yourself. I prefer to read my solo texts aloud. Somehow, for me, to hear the text helps me to relate to it. Use your Bible to reinforce the scripture lesson in the text. Read the entire chapter that the text comes from—or even better, read the entire book! How can you enable your soloist to tell the story if you have no idea what the story is?

When you introduce the text to your soloists, spend a few

minutes talking about the text. Ask them to study the text and to read any corresponding scripture lessons you may have found in your study as valuable insights. At your next rehearsal, encourage a discussion between you and your soloist about the text. Share personal faith stories and scriptures that the text may have brought to mind.

Why is this personal interpretation so important? This solo should be an act of worship, praise, celebration, prayer, sorrow, petition—whatever the text brings out in the soloist. When a text is approached in this manner, the work takes on a life of its own, the Spirit of God begins to flow through your singer in a new way, and the song becomes worship!

A great place to start learning how to "preach the story" is with a solo that tells the story through the experience of a specific character. In chapter 2, I mentioned John Horman's anthem, "The Lost Sheep." I highlighted the fact that an adult sings this anthem in the character of a shepherd. This Bible story is so familiar to us that a "beginner" soloist would be able to convey the story through the character with only a minimum of time spent discussing the text. Also consider using some of the ethnic hymns and spirituals in your hymnal to enable your soloist to "get into" the story. "O Mary, Don't You Weep" (UMH No. 134) is referenced to John 20:11-18 and Exodus 15:21. The joy found in the verse is universal to all Christians and the Bible reference will help your soloist understand and tell the story.

Now that your soloist understands the text, what can you do to help the singer use his or her technique and musicianship to "preach" it?

Musical Skills and Techniques to "Preach" It

In preparing to work with your soloist, compare the musical line and phrasing and the text line and phrasing. Do they work together? Do you feel the text phrase and the musical line the same way that the composer did? Try the phrasing and musical line several different ways.

There are literally hundreds of arrangements of Psalm 23. Each one emphasizes the text in a slightly different way.

Say each of these lines, emphasizing the italicized word.

The *Lord* is my shepherd, I *shall* not want.

The Lord is *my* shepherd, *I* shall not want.

The Lord is my *shepherd,* I shall *not* want.

The Lord is *my* shepherd, I shall *not want.*

Each of these conveys a slightly different meaning. I practice doing just this with the texts of my solo works and underline the words that I wish to emphasize or that I want to be the "top" of the musical phrase. Breath and break marks can also be used to emphasize a text. The minutest silence between a word or phrase can tell the story also. This is of incredible importance when your soloist is serving as the cantor chanting on a psalm tone.

In choral rehearsals, we spend much time working on vowel sounds and consonants. Now you will need to spend an equal amount of time using vowels and consonants to tell the story. Sing the following phrases in a *legato* (smooth) style on any comfortable pitch, in the manner of a chant. Remember to emphasize or stress the italicized words to "preach" the story.

The *Lord* is my shepherd, I *shall* not want.

The Lord is *my* shepherd, *I* shall not want.

The Lord is my *shepherd,* I shall *not* want.

The Lord is *my* shepherd, I shall *not want.*

Do you see how vowels and consonants work together to tell the story? You quickly discovered that you needed to emphasize some consonants more than others to get across the meaning in the variety of ways listed. Use these same techniques to enable the soloist to be able to understand the importance of the use of consonants, vowels, and stress to tell the story. Consider the word *shepherd*. Try singing this word on one pitch in a variety of ways. Proclaim it! Soften it as if a lullaby. Accent the first syllable. Now accent only the second syllable. Accent them evenly. How does the length of the consonants change as you change the way you sing the word? Did you realize how much consonants can help you tell the story beyond just emphasizing proper diction?

The singer is not alone in preaching the story. The accompaniment and the relationship between the accompanist and the singer are also of vital importance! The accompanist should listen for the musical phrase and text emphasis of the soloist and use the accompaniment to support and enhance the work. Listen for places where the accompaniment matches the melodic line or creates a countermelody to the original melody and bring this out. Listen for the rise and fall of the phrase and for the places where the soloist is taking a breath. Decide if you should lift with the soloist or carry over the phrase. Make sure that the organ registration or touch on the piano matches the mood and message of the text. All of these are equally important whether the singer is new to solo singing or has had a professional solo career. Now, we're talking about preaching the story of God!

I had just taken a bite of a gooey, yummy chili hot dog during a break at Annual Conference when a man walked up to me and asked, "How do you get us to sing together?" Unable to reply with my mouth full, I'm sure the look on my face must have registered surprise because he backtracked and started again. "I mean, how do you manage to let us know how we are to sing the hymn without moving your arms or telling us in advance?" I honestly hadn't thought about it.

It wasn't until the next fall when I was teaching my children's choir Helen Kemp's famous phrase "Body, mind, spirit, voice. It takes a whole person to sing and rejoice!" that I started to put together the answer.

If we are to truly praise God, we are to let God's Spirit fill our whole bodies, not just our vocal chords or fingers and feet. How can you sing "O For a Thousand Tongues to Sing" with slumped shoulders, lowered eyes, and a glum look on your face? What can we learn from preachers about how to tell the story? Look at their faces and body language. What does your body language say about what you believe? Does your body language match what you are "preaching" or telling through the solo?

I am not suggesting that you add body movement. I am suggesting that the soloist's facial expression and body posture reflect the message of the story. Look at each verse individually and decide together with your soloist what the soloist's body language should reflect. This is not something many people do automatically, but anyone can be taught to be sensitive to this issue.

Practice Makes Perfect!

"Can you fit in an extra lesson with me? I just found out that I have a solo to sing in two weeks!"

Shame, shame on that director of music! In chapter 2, I highlighted the need to plan in advance to allow these skills to take "hold" in the soloists' bodies. Preaching the story adds even more to absorb on top of all of the vocal techniques the soloist is trying to incorporate into his or her singing. It takes time to make all of these techniques comfortable to the point that your soloist can truly be involved in telling the story, in preaching the Word through music. No one is able to do the best job possible without time to practice and to grow with the piece of music! I simply cannot emphasize that strongly enough.

What are some of the most often repeated pitfalls church music leaders fall into?

"Just look at me and I'll nod when it's time to come in."
All soloists can learn to listen and count, even if they don't
read music. You need to work together to have a sense of the
message. One way to let the vocalist practice and become comfortable with entrances is to record the accompaniment (for
rehearsal purposes only) and to encourage your singer to practice with the tape at home. My singers pop the tape into the
cassette player in their car and sing along on the way to and
from work.

"You can learn it in one rehearsal. Just stay after choir
rehearsal and I'll teach it to you." First of all, they probably
can't learn it in one rehearsal, especially after they've worked
so hard for you in your choir rehearsal. Face facts! Your
singers' voices, energy, and brains are tired after singing one
and a half to two hours. They will not be able to get it all
together when "running on empty." Set aside a few rehearsals
when your singer (and you) are fresh. Use after-choir times for
quick refresher run-throughs only.

"Listen to this tape and learn it from the tape." Yes, listening to a good performance of the work will help your soloist get
a grasp of the total work, and it can help. However, a tape is
not a teacher, enabler, or encourager! I was asked to accompany on the piano a young singer for a local scholarship competition. I went over the tempo, music markings, breath markings,
and so on with her and then began the introduction. She didn't
come in! I started again, but not a peep out of her! Finally, I
asked her what was going on, and she replied, "I'm waiting to
hear the flutes play the line before I come in." Unless you are
planning to hire the entire orchestra or whatever is on the
accompaniment on the taped performance, most singers will
have to make the adjustment to hearing organ, piano, or whatever instrumentation is used in the actual accompaniment. This
takes practice! Finding the pitch in your voice against a guitar is
different from finding the pitch in your voice against a piano.

I asked, "What would you do differently when singing this for a concert or as part of a worship service?" The role of a solo in worship is not to entertain, to fill in a Sunday for the choir, or to get the director of music off the hook because of poor planning. The role of a solo is to enable the listeners to be open to be renewed, refreshed, and reborn in God's way. Again, I say to you, when a solo is approached in this manner, the solo takes on a life of its own, the Spirit of God begins to flow through your singer in a new way, and the song becomes worship!

Chapter Seven
Ministry Matters!

I f you are a director of music in a local church the ministry of music involves YOU! Yes, ministry matters! Many years ago, I considered myself a director of music, and that's exactly what I did! I directed music. I look back over some of my years in the local church and regret the many times when I missed the opportunity to minister to and with the members of my choirs and church. I was much more concerned about the performance than the person. I believed that the performance was the most important goal of my work. I have discovered since then that when putting the person and ministry first, the performance goes to incredible heights I only dreamed about before.

How and why did this happen? One of the persons God used in my life was someone who wasn't even a member of my church. Chick was a member of a neighboring Methodist church and the father of one of my adult choir members. After his retirement, he joined my bell choir and instrumental ensemble, played trombone solos, and sang solos because he loved the Lord so much that he wanted to continually express that love in new ways. (His choir director and I worked out when he would be where!) He taught me so much about ministry. Even after being diagnosed with cancer, he was there for me until he wasn't physically able to do it anymore, and even then he came and listened and mouthed the words. He would always tell me as he left rehearsals, "I've got you in my prayers, you know." I joined his family as we sang hymns and songs around Chick's hospital bed the night he died, and as we sang I realized that I had become a participant in ministry together with Chick during those last few years together. Chick is one of those in my life for whom I sing, "For all the saints!"

When this change happened in me, I began to search for what God wanted me to do with my life in a whole new way. My search and God's call took me to a new understanding of ministry and to new places in my ministry. My personal search led me to diaconal ministry; I am now a consecrated diaconal minister in The United Methodist Church. Your search for the place God is calling may take you down a different path, but you will begin to see why I believe that working one-on-one with your singers is so valuable.

The Ministry of Caring for Your Singer

Will working on a piece give your soloist a sense of achievement or fear? The solo you have given to your singers tells them that you have confidence in their ability and that you believe they have something to offer in worship. If the piece is out of their reach, they will not feel good about what they have to offer. They will not be able to preach or tell the story with confidence! On the other hand, a well-chosen work, that has been a challenge that they were able to meet will reinforce their belief in themselves and their part in telling the story of God.

Two questions you will want to ask yourself are:

1. Is this the right piece for this singer? Consider all of the issues this book has raised; text, range, vocal skill, musical skill, and overall difficulty of the piece. Consider also how much time your singer will need to learn the work and plan accordingly.

2. Does this piece present too much of a challenge or not enough? Only you are able to judge the growth of musical skills and musicality in your singer. Consider this wisely.

3. Finally, will this piece enable your soloist to feel as
though he or she has added to worship and has been
able to offer the gift of singing to the best of his or her
ability?

The ministry of caring for your choir and church members
involves relationships. Not just the relationship between you
and your singer, but between the singer and God. Have you
enabled your singers to join in with all of God's creation as they
praise God? "Let everything that has breath praise the Lord!"

Ministry to Others Through Music

Why was I considered a part of Chick's family? I think it
was because we had spent time together one-on-one working
on his solos. We'd practice a little, talk and share together,
practice a little, talk and share, practice. I kept up with what
was happening in his life and in his family's life through this
time together. I was able to share in his joys and his sorrows.
We were able to pray together. There is something special
about creating music for worship together. The Spirit of God
binds you together as you work together on making the solo
the best that it can be.

The time spent working with your soloist is so important to
relationship building. You have a chance to talk with him and
really get to know him! You can finally figure out who he is
related to in the church, and hear about his job, his family, and
his concerns and opinions about the music ministry.

What you share together will be built upon week to week.
You will need to continue asking about your singer and her
family: Is her mom feeling better? Is the chicken pox making
the rounds in the house? Did her daughter pass her bar exam?
and so forth. Call during the week and follow up on these concerns. If it is appropriate, share with your pastor and other
members of the church staff this person's concerns and joys.

If you listen to and hear their everyday kinds of joys and concerns, your soloists will call you and share with you the times when their lives really get rough or at the high points in their lives. Your singers will learn to trust you and you will be able to share with them the ministry of music.

A member of my children's choir wrote to me: "You make music a heart form!" Now, I'm not sure if she meant "art" form or "heart" form, but I think that "heart form" says a lot! Trust is a key word in music ministry. Your soloists will need to learn that they can trust you and that you will be honest with them. Remember, music is a "heart form" and you will need to share together in the making of music. They are trusting you with the choice of music and they are trusting you to enable them to do the best they can in worship. They will also learn to trust and share with you in times of sorrow and joy in their lives as one of their leaders in their faith community.

When spending time helping your soloists learn, you are also ministering to your faith community by enabling one of them to become a leader in the church. Look at your choir. The members are probably among the most active members in your church. They certainly are among the most dedicated! As your soloists gain self-confidence and a sense of self-value by preparing to lead in worship by singing a solo, they are also being prepared to be a committee chair or a lay reader, or for just about any position in the church.

You are ministering to the total music ministry of your church as you work with and teach each of your choir members to improve their singing ability. This is the perfect way to improve the singing of your choir—you are just doing it one person at a time. Think of all the possibilities of musical concepts that could be taught in this special time with your singers. Now think of what your choir could sound like, as each singer begins to improve and sing to the best of his or her ability individually.

As you work with your solo singers, teach them the how's and why's of music. Offer to bring in resource materials! Many members of my choir have worked their way through a very basic music theory book. Your choir can learn music theory, one singer at a time. You will find that you won't have to correct vowel sounds or consonants or rhythms as often in choir rehearsal. Your choir will be more sensitive to dynamics and musical phrasing and musical style. The choir will begin to hear the improved sound and this will help them to begin to challenge themselves to be the best that they can be.

A support system will be built within your choir for one another as each person shares his or her gift. Your choir will begin to share together as each gives to worship the best that he or she can. Each person becomes a valuable presence in the choir, whether your choir has 7 members or 30 members or 137 members. The appreciation of one another's offerings to God will also grow to include appreciation for their presence at choir rehearsal and worship. This leadership training is an important way to minister to one another through music in the local church choir.

Called to Ministry

You have read my story of one of the turning points in my faith life. I believe that as you involve yourself in the enabling process, you too, will have a turning point. Each person has been given a gift by God! Read again the words of 1 Corinthians 12:4-11.

> Now there are varieties of gifts, but the same Spirit; and there are varieties of services, but the same Lord; and there are varieties of activities, but it is the same God who activates all of them in everyone. To each is given the manifestation of the Spirit for the common good. To one is given through the Spirit the utterance of wisdom, and to another the utterance of

knowledge according to the same Spirit, to another faith by the same Spirit, to another gifts of healing by the one Spirit, to another the working of miracles, to another prophecy, to another the discernment of spirits, to another various kinds of tongues, to another the interpretation of tongues. All these are activated by one and the same Spirit, who allots to each one individually just as the Spirit chooses.

What did I do with those three singers who introduced themselves to me as the section soloists my first night of choir rehearsal? I asked them to sing duets with someone else to help that person learn from them about how to sing. I encouraged them to become the enablers and to understand that all of us have a gift to share.

I believe that God calls those in music leadership to help and enable those persons in our music ministry and our church to develop these gifts to the fullest measure. Have you enabled your music ministry members to develop their gifts to the fullest measure? Have you enabled your soloists to use their gifts to the fullest measure? As the music leader in your church you are called to use the gift of teaching to help others learn how to praise and worship God. Solos and soloists are a gift from God for us all to share in worship and to praise the Creator of all music! Use this gift wisely and your ministry will be blessed.

Selected Bibliography

Scripture Cross-Reference Books for Sacred Solos

Soloist's Guide to Selecting Sacred Solos. Designed, compiled, and edited by Joan Welles. The Soloists Guide, P.O. Box 55043, Indianapolis, IN 46205. (Over 650 sacred solos uniquely indexed for easy access by title, composer, biblical reference, topic, publisher, and range.)

Vocal Solos for Christian Churches, 3rd ed. Noni Espina. The Scarecrow Press, Inc., Metuchen, N.J., and London, 1984. (A descriptive reference of solo music for the church year including a bibliographical supplement of choral works.)

Books on Diction

The Singer's Manual of English Diction. Madeleine Marshall. Schirmer Books, 1953. *The* book of basic diction for singers.

English Diction for the Singer. Lloyd Pfautsch. Lawson-Gould Music Publishers, 1971. *The* (other) book of basic diction for singers.